AF613600

Table of Contents

Introduction

Since Airbnb was established in 2007 (and launched three times before it found success), it has grown to a true phenomenon. Its vast listings and unique quality help it to rival the hotel industry, which often can't compete with the at-home feeling you can get in an Airbnb. Travelers interested in short-term to long-term accommodation have an incredible number of worldwide options. You can grab everything from a private room in a larger house up to a premium apartment for a business trip. Of course, Airbnbs aren't always perfect, but it's all part of the experience. Airbnb is an online marketplace and hospitality service, aiding users to rent or lease accommodation not limited to bed and breakfasts, hostels, homestays, apartments, rooms, or hotels. Airbnb does not own any of the properties but collects brokerage fee and service fee percentages from both the host and the guest per booking. Airbnb was established in August of 2008 and founded in San Francisco, California. Accommodations located all over the world can be booked online using a tablet, mobile phone, PC, or Mac. Airbnb is an innovative business that has grown faster than anyone could have imagined, in fact, it has been dubbed as the world's fastest-growing travel website! It has shifted the travel paradigm in a new direction, satisfying consumer desires to take part in the sharing economy and reducing travel costs.

What is Airbnb?

Airbnb is essentially an online marketplace that involves the renting of property to travelers. They have also recently started offering experiences too. Airbnb does not own any of the properties. It simply provides a platform from which people can rent out their properties or spare rooms to guests. Prices are set by the property owners and monies are collected via the Airbnb app.

The history of Airbnb

Airbnb founders Joe Gebbia, Brian Chesky, and Nathan Blecharczyk developed the business in 2008. Initially, Gebbia and Chesky started off using their own place as a bed-and-breakfast to make a few extra bucks to pay rent. With a big design conference coming to the San Francisco area and a city full of sold-out hotels at the time, they saw a potential market for the idea and developed a website called airbedandbreakfast.com. To fund their operation, the guys sold breakfast cereals during the 2008 presidential race — Obama O's and Cap'n McCains — and the cereals earned them around $30,000.Airbnb was not an immediate success, though. The startup experienced several ups and downs, and it went through at least three separate launches. Several investors didn't take the idea seriously. However, one venture capitalist, Paul Graham, did see a potential lottery ticket in Air Bed & Breakfast. Graham invited the founders to join a program called Y Combinator, which provides a startup with cash and training in exchange for a percentage of their company. In 2009, Air Bed & Breakfast became Airbnb, and that was the company's turning point. While Airbnb has lost some value in 2020 (along with other hospitality ventures), the company has filed an IPO to go public after delaying the decision once in 2019.

How Airbnb works: Making a booking

It’s incredibly simple to get started with an Airbnb vacation. The process works almost like booking a hotel room, though some homeowners have verification processes where they can approve your rental. So long as you don’t have previous bad reviews, you shouldn’t have any problem. Here’s a quick look at the steps involved:

- Sign up.
- Find a place you love at your destination.
- Check the details.
- Make a booking and wait for the host to accept.
- If the host offers an Instant Book listing, you'll be accepted instantly.

Let's break each step down further.

Sign up for Airbnb

Signing up to Airbnb involves registering as a guest, and entering the required data. Note that you will go through a verification process as well, so take your time and get the information right the first time. In particular, your phone number will be crucial for Airbnb to contact you via text message. You will also have to sign an agreement where treat every person equally, regardless of race, gender, religion, or other factors, which is a big part of the Airbnb culture. It should be part of everyone's culture, but good on Airbnb for enforcing it. You also have the option of signing up through a linked Facebook or Google account, though it may be easiest to just use email. Airbnb offers the occasional coupon as well, so you might want to check with family and friends.

Find an Airbnb you love

Browsing for stays is extremely simple on Android, iOS, and even web browsers. You simply load up the app or webpage and search for where you want to go. When Airbnb started, you could only filter by entire homes or private rooms. Private rooms are often part of a home and are a cheap way to grab a bunk. An Entire Place will offer the apartment or house or sometimes unique destinations like houseboats or buses all to yourself. However, you can now filter by more key features like pet friendliness, unique stays, and moreLike any vacation service, Airbnb is all about location, location, location. You'll want to know if you need a car to get to the destination, or if public transportation will suffice. Sometimes hosts will mention they can pick you up and drive you to your destination, which is a nice touch. As always, knowing even a little bit of information about your destination can really help you decide. Places further away from main tourist hotspots are often cheaper, and sometimes they're just an easy bus or train ride away. Once you find a stay that looks interesting, be sure to go through all of the available pictures. They'll mainly show you the best angles of the house or room, but it's good to know what you're getting into.

Check the listing details

This is just a matter of reading the entire Airbnb listing and ensuring you know all the details. Some listings require that you bring your own bedding, or say check-in is only available at unusual times. Double-check everything before booking, check the reviews, and just make sure you know the catches like strict cancellation fees. All the other fees add up too, so be careful. Misreading the listing details is one of the main ways that things can go wrong in an Airbnb. You might expect an entire home to yourself and then be surprised when the homeowner shows up.

Make a booking and wait for the host to accept

You can message the Airbnb host in advance to clarify details about the listing, but otherwise, you can click through to make a booking and send a little note as

Airbnb prompts. The homeowner should hopefully send a confirmation within a few hours, depending on the respective time zones.

how Airbnb works for hosts

Airbnb has different hosting options — you can rent out the extra space in your home, you can rent out your entire home, or you can host experiences in your area. To rent out extra space in your home, you must first create a free Airbnb account. Then, you click on "become a host" in the upper right-hand corner of the page. After that, you'll need to create a listing for your space. A listing is a lot like a profile page for the space you want to host; just like a social media profile, the nicer your page looks, the more attention it will draw. It's a good idea to make your space look as nice as possible and take flattering pictures of the space. How much should you charge? Airbnb helps you set the pricing by indicating the averages for your area. You can also make money on Airbnb by hosting an experience. "Airbnb Experiences are activities designed and led by inspiring locals. They go beyond typical tours or classes by immersing guests in a host's unique world," says the Airbnb site. If you want to host an experience, review Airbnb's quality standards, which indicate requirements for experiences. Basically, the guest must be gaining access to something, participating in something, and offered an original perspective. After reviewing the quality standards, design your experience and submit it to Airbnb for approval. Once approved, you are ready to publish and host your experience.

Positive impacts of Airbnb

Whilst there has been a growing body of public literature that views the use of Airbnb and the wider sharing economy as negative in terms of its impacts, particularly economically, there are also some positive impacts of Airbnb.

Airbnb encourages economic activity in communities that wouldn’t normally benefit from tourism

Many Airbnb accommodations are in areas away from the usual tourist hot spots. I have stayed in rural areas of Costa Rica, inner-city Cape Town, and in a suburban apartment in Calgary, for example. This can help to bring much-needed income to areas that otherwise would not benefit from tourism. Whether it's from buying your tea at the local supermarket or going out for dinner in a restaurant around the corner, tourists typically spend money in the vicinity of their accommodation location.

Airbnb saves the traveler money

Most people know that Airbnb can save the traveler money, which is one of the biggest motivating factors for opting to use the company when choosing their accommodation options. Airbnb accommodations can cost a fraction of the price of a traditional hotel or other accommodation option serviced by the tourism industry.

Airbnb allows travelers to learn about the local communities

As I pointed out earlier in this article, Airbnb provides travelers with a more authentic and local experience because they are living with locals or staying in local communities.

Airbnb provides an income to people who need it

Airbnb has welcomed many entrepreneurs and businessmen and women into the sharing economy industry. It has allowed people to make an income when they may have previously been unable to. This can provide economic benefits to marginalized communities, impoverished areas, and people experiencing economic hardship, which is particularly prevalent in developing countries.

Negative impacts of Airbnb

Unfortunately, there are also many negative impacts of Airbnb, namely economic impacts. According to the Economic Policy Institute, the costs of Airbnb businesses are likely to outweigh the benefits. Here are some of the negative impacts that have been noted:

Airbnb causes increases in housing costs

Airbnb can be a big revenue earner. Once homeowners begin to realize this, they are likely to snap up further properties in the same, or alternative, locations. The increases in demand for properties raise the prices, it's simple supply and demand theory.

Airbnb enhances the likelihood of gentrification

Because the price of property goes up, many local people begin to be pushed out. People can longer afford the accommodation available to them in the area that they live in and are therefore forced to relocate to cheaper areas.

It is more difficult to collect taxes from Airbnb stays than from traditional hotel transactions

Another economic impact of Airbnb is the difficulty in collecting taxes. Traditional tourism accommodation providers are subject to a range of tax laws, from employment taxes on cleaners and cooks to city taxes. It is a lot more difficult to collect taxes from Airbnb providers. This loss in revenue means that there is less money in the pot for community investments in areas such as healthcare or education, therefore having a knock-on effect on the overall welfare of the community.

Airbnb guests may be unwanted in local communities

Some local communities may not welcome Airbnb guests. Tourists may be ignorant to local customs, for example by wearing revealing clothing in a Muslim country or by swearing in the street. Tourists may be inconsiderate to neighbors by playing loud music or by littering. Tourists may flaunt expensive gadgets and jewelry that the locals cannot afford, therefore encouraging feelings of resentment and perhaps even rises in crime. In fact, many of the wider negative social impacts of tourism, in general, can be applied to smaller communities that house Airbnb properties.

There are privacy and safety concerns with Airbnb

Lastly, there have been several concerns over the privacy and safety of Airbnb. From hidden cameras to doors that don't lock properly, there have been many reported complaints from Airbnb and guests throughout the world. Although the review system should help to reduce such incidents, unfortunately, this does not always seem to be the case.

Wide Selection

Airbnb hosts list many different kinds of properties—single rooms, a suite of rooms, apartments, moored yachts, houseboats, entire houses, even a castle—on the Airbnb website.

Free Listings

Hosts don't have to pay to list their properties. Listings can include written descriptions, photographs with captions, and a user profile where potential guests can get to know a bit about the hosts.

Hosts Can Set Their Own Price

It's up to each host to decide how much to charge per night, per week, or month.

Customizable Searches

Guests can search the Airbnb database—not only by date and location, but by price, type of property, amenities, and the language of the host. They can also add keywords (such as “close to the Louvre”) to further narrow their search.

Additional Services

In recent years Airbnb has expanded its offerings to include experiences and restaurants. Besides a listing of available accommodations for the dates they plan to travel, people searching by location will see a list of experiences, such as classes and sightseeing, offered by local Airbnb hosts. Restaurant listings also include reviews from Airbnb hosts.

Protections for Guests and Hosts

As a protection for guests, Airbnb holds the guest's payment for 24 hours after check-in before releasing the funds to the host. For hosts, Airbnb's Host Guarantee program "protects up to $1,000,000 in damages to covered property in the rare event of guest damage, in eligible countries."

What You See May Not Be What You Get

Booking accommodations with Airbnb is not like booking a room with a major hotel chain, where you have a reasonable assurance that the property will be as advertised. Individual hosts create their own listings, and some may be more honest than others. However, previous guests often post comments about their experiences, which can provide a more objective view.

Potential Damage

Probably the biggest risk for hosts is that their property will be damaged. While most stays go without incident, there are stories of entire houses being trashed by dozens of partygoers when the Airbnb hosts thought they were renting to a quiet family. Airbnb's Host Guarantee program, described above, provides some assurance, but it may not cover everything, such as cash, rare artwork, jewelry, and pets. Hosts whose homes are damaged may also experience considerable inconvenience.

Added Fees

Airbnb imposes several additional fees (as, of course, do hotels and other lodging providers). Guests pay a guest service fee of 0% to 20% on top of the reservation fee, to cover Airbnb's customer support and other services. Prices displayed in the currency the user selects provided Airbnb supports it. Banks or credit card issuers may add fees if applicable. And while listings are free, Airbnb charges hosts a service fee of at least 3% for each reservation, to cover the cost of processing the transaction.

Taxes

Both hosts and guests from the European Union, Switzerland, and Norway may be subject to a value-added tax (VAT). And depending on their location, hosts may be subject to rental income taxes. To assist with U.S. tax compliance, Airbnb collects taxpayer information from hosts so they can provide an account of their earnings each year via Form 1099 and Form 1042.

It Isn't Legal Everywhere

Before listing their properties on Airbnb, would-be hosts need to check their local zoning ordinances to make sure it's legal to rent out their properties. Hosts may also be required to obtain special permits or licenses.

Cancellations Due to COVID-19

On March 11, 2020, the World Health Organization declared a global pandemic due to the novel coronavirus. In response, Airbnb adjusted its extenuating circumstances cancellation policy on March 14. The newest adjustment was made on October 1. Reservations booked on or before March 14 with a check-in date within the next 45 days from today are eligible for a full refund for coronavirus-related reasons. To facilitate this, Airbnb has set aside a fund of $250 million that will be used to help hosts impacted by the cancellations, paying them 25% of what they would have received for a normal cancellation. Reservations made after March 14 are not eligible for this policy and subject to standard cancellation procedures. Reservations made before March 14 but with a check-in date within the next 45 days from today will be revisited as the policy is updated. The new policy "doesn't apply to Airbnb Luxe, Luxury Retreats, or domestic bookings in mainland China, which all have their own policies." Airbnb has set aside a $10 million support fund to assist "our community in mainland China directly."

Airbnb runs an online marketplace for short-term lodging rentals. It largely does not own dwellings or real estate of its own; instead, it collects fees by acting as a broker between those with dwellings to rent and those looking to book lodging. The perception that Airbnb tries to foster is that its "hosts" are relatively typical households looking to earn supplementary income by renting out rooms in their homes or by renting out their entire residence when they're away. Critics argue that Airbnb bookings have become increasingly concentrated among a relatively small number of "hosts" that are essentially miniature hotel companies.

Potential economic benefits

At a broad level, the potential economic benefits and costs of Airbnb are relatively straightforward. The key potential benefit is that property owners can diversify the potential streams of revenue they generate from owning homes. Say, for example, that before Airbnb arrived in a city, property owners setting up residential rental properties faced transaction costs so high that it only made economic sense to secure relatively long-term leases. These transaction costs incurred by property owners could include advertising for and screening tenants and finding alternative accommodations for themselves if they were renting their own dwellings. But if the rise of internet-based service firms reduced these transaction costs and made short-term rentals logistically feasible and affordable for the first time, it could allow these property owners to diversify into short-term rentals as well as long-term rentals.

Another potential benefit is the increased supply (and variety) of short-term rentals available to travelers. This increased supply can restrain price growth for short-term rentals and make traveling more affordable.

Finally, one well-advertised potential benefit of Airbnb is the extra economic activity that might result if the rise of Airbnb spurs an increase in visitors to a city or town. Besides the income generated by Airbnb property owners, income might be generated by these visitors as they spend money at restaurants or in grocery stores, or on other activities.

Potential costs The single biggest potential cost imposed by Airbnb comes in the form of higher housing costs for city residents if enough properties are converted from long-term housing to short-term accommodations. If property owners take dwellings that were available for long-term leases and convert them to short-term Airbnb listings, this increases the supply of short-term rentals (hence driving down their price) but decreases the supply of long-term housing, increasing housing costs for city residents. (We refer to all long-term costs of shelter as "housing," including rentals and owners' equivalent rental costs.)Another large potential city-specific cost of Airbnb expansion is the loss of tax revenue. Many cities impose relatively steep taxes on short-term lodging, hoping to obtain revenue from out-of-town travelers to spend on residents. The most common and straightforward of these revenue raisers is a tax on traditional hotel rooms. If Airbnb expansion comes at the expense of traditional hotels, and if the apparatus for collecting taxes from Airbnb or its hosts is less well-developed than the apparatus for collecting taxes from traditional hotels, this could harm city revenues. A further potential cost is the externalities that property rentals (of all kinds) impose on neighbors, for example, noise and/or use of building facilities. Since hosts are often not on-site with their renters, they do not bear the costs of these externalities and hence may not factor them into rental decisions. Of course, one could argue that such externalities are also incurred with long-term rentals not arranged through Airbnb. But if the expansion of Airbnb increases total short- and long-term rental activity, or if short-term rentals impose larger externalities than long-term rentals, then Airbnb expansion can increase these externalities. Finally, if Airbnb expansion comes at the expense of traditional hotels, it could hurt employment. First, since some of the labor of maintaining Airbnb lodgings is performed by the property owners themselves, the shift to Airbnb from traditional hotels would actually reduce employment overall. Second, since the task of cleaning and maintaining rooms and even greeting Airbnb renters is often done by third-party management firms, the shift from the traditional hotel sector to Airbnb rentals could degrade job quality.

The rest of this report evaluates the potential scope of each of these benefits and costs and ends with an overall assessment of the effect of Airbnb expansion.

Is Airbnb safe?

Unfortunately, there are some bad apples in the Airbnb industry, both hosts and guests. From hosts placing meth pipes in their accommodation and watching guests on hidden cameras, to guests using the accommodation as a brothel and having huge parties, Airbnb is not without its fair share of dramas. Fortunately, horror stories like these are not common, and most people have a perfectly pleasant and safe stay in their Airbnb accommodation! In fact, Airbnb has several measures in place to ensure safety for their guests. This includes risk scoring, background and watchlist checks, handing out free carbon monoxide and smoke detectors to hosts, having a secure payment platform, and a multi-layer defense strategy to prevent scams.

conclusion

As you can see throughout this book, Airbnb is a groundbreaking company that has seen incredible growth in a short period of time. A prominent name in the sharing economy, Airbnb has become a household name. Despite being remarkably popular with travelers and hosts alike, however, it has not been without its critics. Many academics and industry professionals have raised concerns over the sustainability of Airbnb, with negative economic impacts demonstrated the world over. Despite this, the company and its competitors continue to grow and to increase their share of the accommodation market.

www.ingramcontent.com/pod-product-compliance
Ingram Content Group UK Ltd.
Pitfield, Milton Keynes, MK11 3LW, UK
UKHW021925190726
13853UKWH00002B/850

9 798417 456800